30 BEST KETTLEBELL WORKOUTS

Kettlebell Exercises for body fitness, Boost Muscles, Stretching, and build full-body strength.

GYMMESS PRESSY

TABLE OF CONTENTS

INTRODUCTION

Kettlebells are excellent strength equipment. They may be used in place of dumbbells or other weight instruments for a certain workout. Kettlebells, on the other hand, is rated high for certain weighted movements, especially those that necessitate an explosive action.

They are much simpler to swing around because of their form. You may also catch them by the stick or the bell (the round portion of the weight), giving you a wider range of motion based on the kettlebell workout. A kettlebell's form allows you to work your muscles in a unique manner than a typical dumbbell.

In this book, you will learn different types of exercises that you can use the kettlebell to do and also how you can achieve your body fitness, full-body workout, and building strength with the kettlebell.

Kettlebells are among the most versatile as well as powerful fitness equipment around, and as this year's results show, people adore them and deem them indispensable.

PART 1: BASIC UNDERSTANDING OF KETTLEBELL EXERCISES

A kettlebell has the shape of a cannonball made of cast iron with a top handle. They are accessible in a range of weights. You will need them for full-body fitness, lifts, as well as shoulder presses, and other movements.

The routine exercises with kettlebell raise or increase your heartbeat rate (which is normal in all forms of exercise) and burn up to 20 to 30 calories per minute, which is equivalent to doing a 6-minute mile exercise.

WHAT IS KETTLEBELL?

A kettlebell is a form of cycle shape that looks like a ball produced or made with cast iron or steel with a handle tied to the end (looks like a cannonball with a handle). It's used for a variety of workouts, particularly ballistic workouts that incorporate cardio, agility, including flexibility. In the weightlifting sport or fitness of kettlebell lifting, they are the main equipment being used.

Kettlebell routines are highly flexible. You can incorporate a couple of the exercises into your routine or do a weekly kettlebell routine.

BRIEF HISTORY:

In the 18th century, the Russian girya was a type of metal weight that was mainly used to measure crops. The use of these weights by circus authoritarian leaders is known years back to the nineteenth century. During the late 1800s, they were first used in Russia as well as Europe for leisure and competitive strength athletics. Intensive kettlebell lifting, also called girevoy sport, years back to 1885 when the "Circle for Amateur Sports" was created.

The weight of a Russian girya is usually weighed in poods, which equals 16.38 kilograms. Since before the early twentieth century, the English word kettlebell is mostly used.

The haltere, which was comparable to the contemporary kettlebell in form of movements, was a weight used during Classical Greece.

SHAPES:

Indian clubs or ishi sashi have a center of mass that extends beyond the wrist, unlike conventional dumbbells. Ballistic as well as swinging movements are made easier as a result of this. Bags filled with sand, water, including steel shot are among the kettlebell's varieties. The kettlebell makes for safer swing and releases motions, as well as increased grasp, hand, shoulder, and core strength.

A kettlebell's weight is not uniformly spread. As a result, a kettlebell's unusual structure provides "unstable energy" for handling, which is critical for the success of kettlebell exercises.

PART 2: BENEFITS OF KETTLEBELL WORKOUTS

The followings are the benefits you will derive from kettlebell routine workouts.

FULL BODY WORKOUTS:

Kettlebells can be used to boost or improve stamina, agility, stability, and balance, which are the four primary components of fitness. This is without a doubt or uncertainty one of the most important advantages of kettlebells. They're adaptable and make life easier and also give the opportunity to do

IMPROVE BALANCING AND BOOST MUSCLES:

You produce force and move in a preset direction as you practice with it. When practicing with kettlebells, you need to maintain control of the movement direction. This necessitates a concerted effort to reinforce the stability of muscles with each action. Your equilibrium would be excellent if you have solid stabilized muscles in both ranges of motion, as well as improved core strength, as we mentioned in one of the advantages of kettlebells above.

INTENSIVE FAT-BURNING:

Swinging a kettlebell will burn up to 30-15 calories per minute, according to an ACE analysis. mostly 25-minute exercise, that's about 400 calories. Furthermore, since kettlebell training for fat loss is always high impact, you will experience an after-burn in a long run. Excess post-exercise oxygen absorption, or EPOC, is the term for this and this means you will keep on burning calories even after you've completed your workout.

CARDIO ALTERNATIVES:

A flexible kettlebell HIIT, as well as metabolic exercise (low weight, high rep, high intensity based workouts), can do an excellent job of burning calories in a limited period. Many people claim it is more effective than fairly constant cardio in terms of losing fat, increasing metabolism, increasing muscle endurance, and enhancing cardiovascular health. The trick is to ensure that your heartbeat rate is elevated during the exercise.

DEVELOP HIP POWER:

Hip strength is vital because it provides mobility and aids in injury prevention. Besides, the hips play a critical part in a variety of physical activities, including leaping, sprinting, and explosively exiting a sporting pose. In strength and speed activities, knowing how to harness hip force is crucial.

MOBILITY AND FLEXIBILITY:

Kettlebells, instead of solo movements, hold the body loose by incorporating movement sequences Kettlebell. movement patterns allow you to regulate momentum, torque, including a range of motion when moving through various planes of motion. Steadily increasing your mobility as well as flexibility. You'll develop a lot of stability as time goes by, and your joints will get more stable and solid.

IMPROVE YOUR JOINT:

Since kettlebell exercises are complex, they necessitate conscious control. By improving the muscles that protect your joints, you can improve joint strength and flexibility.

Furthermore, as previously said, complex kettlebell routines increase joint stability and agility. Kettlebells of light to intermediate weight is also ideal for this.

PART 3: BUYING BEST KETTLEBELLS KETTLEBELL TYPES TO AVOID.

Beginners frequently asked this question; which of the kettlebell should I purchase?. What size of kettlebell weight to purchase?

They are multiple varieties of kettlebells like what to check for when choosing kettlebells? what kettlebell weights do you require? and finally, a few of the brands of quality kettlebells that I suggest that are perfectly good for fitness exercises are all listed below.

TYPES OF KETTLEBELL:

The followings are the best kettlebells that you will love to use:

VINYL KETTLEBELL:

Vinyl kettlebells have the benefit of being considerably less costly than other iron counterparts, in some cases less than half the amount. Since you're going to improve rapidly when you first start practicing, you'll need multiple kettlebells of various weights.

ADJUSTMENT KETTLEBELL:

Kettlebells that can be adjusted or amended and it has decent workout space without taking up a lot of space in your home gym. Some are built to be convenient and easy to transport when traveling. They provide several weight measures of different resistance up to 40 pounds and are encased to keep you fit when exercising.

CAST-IRON KETTLEBELL:

Kettlebells made with heavy cast iron are ergonomically built for a secure grip as well as the best powerful kettlebell exercise.

If you can't curl your fingertips or your full palm completely or fully around the handle of the kettlebell, it's just too tight for you then you need to consider leaving it for another one.

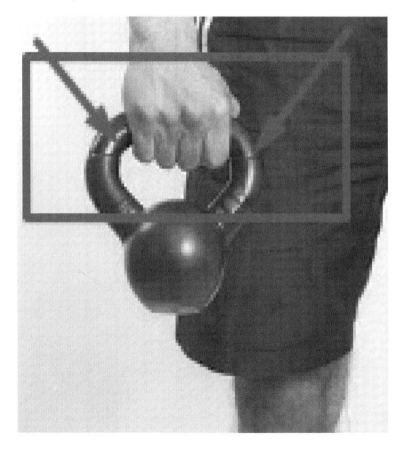

A kettlebell with an overly thick handle can easily wear out the forearms, making completing repetitions of an exercise difficult.

KETTLEBELL HANDLE WIDTH:

First, can you get your hands around the handle of the kettlebell? Any kettlebells, such as those used in sport, are just large enough to accommodate two hands.

You'll need to have a kettlebell that will enable you to get both hands through the handle if you are trying to do a lot of two-handed kettlebell workouts, which I suggest for starters.

FEET AND BASE KETTLEBELL:

The base of the kettlebell ought to be smooth and real, with no rubber or plastic foundation attached, and also it should not be rough.

Bases are useful for avoiding stains on the floor, but they sink into your arm as well as body while you are using the kettlebell.

So, if the kettlebell has a circular rubber or plastic foot, I would steer clear of it.

SHARP KETTLEBELL HANDLE:

The fourth step is to ensure that the kettlebell handle does not have any rough edges.

Kettlebells with sharp pieces of paint should be avoided, and make sure there are no tiny nicks where the handle hits the body that might cut the palms.

If you have a kettlebell that has rough points, you should smooth them down with sandpaper.

ROUND KETTLE BODY:

If it's round, like such a ball, it will bite into your forearm in the bolted position, and the same thing can occur in the top position of the overhead press or kettlebell snatch as well.

And you want a kettlebell with a slightly oval body as well as a handle that fits snugly into the body.

PART 4: 30 KETTLEBELL WORKOUT EXERCISES:

The following are exercises you can do with a kettlebell.

BOTTOM-UP KETTLEBELL PRESS:

- Firstly ensure that you stand straight.
- With your two feet on the floor.
- The kettlebell should be at your front for easy lifting.
- Lift the kettlebell from the floor above your head.
- Lower your arm below your head with the kettlebell.
- Repeat 2-4 times.

KETTLEBELL HALO:

- Firstly ensure that you stand straight.
- With your two feet on the floor.
- The kettlebell should be at your front for easy lifting.
- Pull up the kettlebell with your two hands.
- At the level of your head.

- Rotate the kettlebell around your head.
- Repeat.

KETTLEBELL SQUATTING:

- Firstly ensure that you stand straight.
- With your two feet on the floor.

- The kettlebell should be at your front for easy lifting.
- Pull up the kettlebell with your two hands.
- Lift it while you squat 90 degrees below the floor.
- Raise again and squat.

DEADLIFTS WITH KETTLEBELL:

- Firstly ensure that you stand straight.
- With your two feet on the floor.

- The kettlebell should be at your front for easy lifting.
- Pull up the kettlebell with your two hands from the floor.
- Bend downward 90 degrees down and your face facing front.
- Lift kettlebell and stand straight.
- After that bend down again and stand upward with the kettlebell.
- Repeat.

KETTLEBELL SWING:

- Stand straight with your leg a little bit open.
- The kettlebell should be in the middle between your two legs for easy lifting.
- Bend down up to 90 degrees.
- Swing the kettlebell backward and forward.
- The swinging should pass through your legs

- Repeat the same.

GOBLET PULSE SQUAT:

- Firstly ensure that you stand straight.
- With your two feet on the floor.
- The kettlebell should be at your front for easy lifting.
- lift the kettlebell with your two hands.
- To the level of your chest.
- While you maintain raising and squatting motions. (up and down).
- Repeat the same.

DOUBLE KETTLEBELL FRONT SQUAT:

- This time around with double kettlebells.
- Stand straight with two kettlebells at your front.
- Hold with one hand and the other one with the second hand.
- Lift them at the level of your neck.
- Maintain that posture while you squat downward and upward.
- Continue the process 2-3 times.

TURKISH GETUP:

This multi-part motion takes some repetition and flexibility to learn, but once you get it down, it's a perfect full-body workout. Start with light weights then progressively increase the weights as you advance.

KETTLEBELL CLEAN AND PRESS:

Some other multi-joint movement that powers the whole body is the clean as well as the press. Before pushing straight up, ensure that you keep the weight under control while you clean into the racked spot. Set a timer for 5 to 10 minutes, then switch 5 reps per arm for the duration of the timer.

KETTLEBELL SUITCASE LUNGE:

- First, stand straight with the kettlebell in your hand.
- Hold the handle strong.
- Move one of your legs forward while you kneel with the other side of your leg.
- Stand up
- And repeat the something.

SIT-UP TO PRESS:

- Begin by lying on your back.
- Ensure that your knees are bent and your feet are on the floor.
- In a sit-up motion.
- Hold the kettlebell in hand at the level of your chest.
- Lift the weight outward just as you move up or roll up and then do a sit-up.

SUMO DEADLIFT HIGH PULL:

- Stand straight with your legs are a little bit wide.
- The kettlebell should be on the floor also at the position between your legs.
- Squat down and hold the kettlebell handle with your two hands.
- Raise and lift the kettlebell to the position of your chest.

- Squat again and raise and lift the kettlebell.

HAND TO HAND SWING:

"Use the same type as well as a setup as you will normally use when swinging. The only distinction is that you only use one hand on the handle of the kettlebell at first, then swap hands at the top. Using one of your hands to swings isolates one side at a time, making it less complicated and it improves stability. Since you'll be using one shoulder, you'll need to use a lighter weight than you will for a normal swing.

FIGURE-8s KETTLEBELL:

Figure-8s is one of the most challenging of the drills, according to coach Paul; that's still a lot of fun as well as not too difficult to implement. The hinging action is identical to swinging, except that rather than swinging the bell forward, you move it from the back of the body to the chest with one hand.

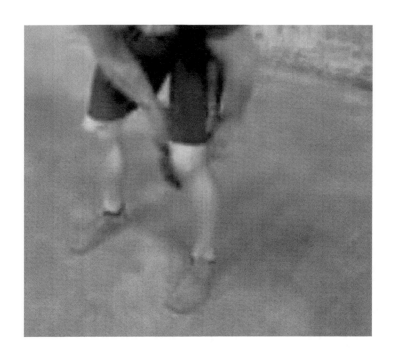

PUSH PRESSES:

- Stand straight on your feet.
- Hold the handle of the kettlebell strong.
- Lift it above your head.
- And down at the level of your chest.
- Repeat the something.

TRICEP PRESSES:

Most people have thin triceps, so you can need to go lighter than with the push presses, according to a fitness coach. Don't curve your back to shield your lower back to ensure you're using your triceps. The trick is to fully straighten your arm at the tip, which will help you to work the triceps across their full range of motion.

BENT-OVER ROW:

- Firstly ensure you stand straight.
- Bend up to 90 degrees.
- Pull the kettlebell up towards your chest.
- Release your hand downward

- Pul again upward.
- Repeat the same.

FUTTER KICK WITH KETTLEBELL:

- Lie straight with your back should be on the floor.
- Hold the kettlebell above your body at an upward level.
- Swing your both legs upward and downward position while you are still holding the kettlebell.

BOX STEPS-UP:

A step-up that strengthens your quads and hip while still strengthening your chest. "There's some instability when you're walking on just one knee, To maintain your body stability, you'll require to use your abs. You'll need a stair, chair, or bench that helps your knee to bend 90 degrees when you step on it for this pass.

FULL BODY KETTLEBELL MOVEMENT:

Performing some of the workout exercises can give you a full-body movement by doing the kettlebell clean, goblet squat, kettlebell thruster, including reverse lunge exercises. Perform four types on 12 reps of all or any of the moves separately, or do them in a circuit with no rest for a total-body exercise.

SINGLE-ARM KETTLEBELL:

Lawrence (coach) once advises, "Position the kettlebell next to your feet." "Capture the kettlebell mostly in your left hand as well as make a huge move back on your left shoulder, leaning your right arm on your right knee. Pull the kettlebell into your hip, gradually lower it until your arm is completely stretched and it reaches the surface. Maintain a set back position throughout."

KETTLEBELL WINDMILL:

This workout improves the core area of your body as well as shoulders while it also increases mobility. With a kettlebell at the right hand, pose with your feet shoulder-width apart. Press the kettlebell completely overhead until another elbow is locked out, turning both feet 45 degrees to the left.

Start by looking up at the weight as well as move your hips to the right while bending over to the left side so your left hand will meet your left foot – or shin if the balance only allows it. Return to your feet and repeat the process. Once you've completed all of the reps on one knee, turn the kettlebell on the other.

KETTLE SQUEEZE:

"Hold the kettlebell to your chest axis, and stretch your arms upward or out in front of you, parallel to the deck. Keep the kettlebell out at the front of you for a second while squeezing your hands as hard as possible, then pull it back in as well as repeat."

DOUBLE THRUSTER KETTLEBELL:

Hold two kettlebells in the rack role when standing with your feet ensure that your hip-width apart. Drop yourself to the ground by bending your legs and sitting your glutes back until your thighs are perpendicular. Hold for a while before exploding into action. When you rise to your feet, press the kettlebells up using the leverage created by the squat to help you. The press should be completed with your palms faced forward. Return the kettlebells to their original rack location.

KETTLEBELL PRESS UP:

"Begin in a press-up stance with your feet together and your hands shoulder-width apart, gripping the kettlebell handles," Lawrence says. "Do a press-up and then a row by lifting your right elbow as well as pressing your shoulder blades mostly together because your elbow comes up past your body at the end of the press-up. Lower as well as row strong with your left hand, then do another press-up to complete the rep."

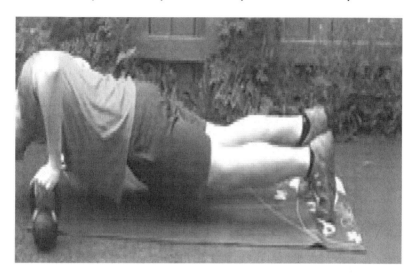

Printed in Great Britain
by Amazon